Marrelle,
May these
offerings lift
your spirits in
these hard times.
Love,
Luisa

ALL THE GIFTS OF LIFE

ALL THE GIFTS OF LIFE

Collected Meditations, Volume Three

COLLECTED BY
PATRICIA FREVERT

SKINNER HOUSE BOOKS
BOSTON

Published by Skinner House Books. Skinner House Books is an imprint of the Unitarian Universalist Association, a liberal religious organization with more than 1,000 congregations in the U.S. and Canada. 25 Beacon St., Boston, MA 02108-2800.

Printed in Canada.

Cover and text design by Suzanne Morgan.

ISBN 1-55896-437-1

Library of Congress Cataloging-in-Publication Data
All the gifts of life / collected by Patricia Frevert.
        p. cm. – (Collected meditations ; vol. 3)
     ISBN 1-55896-437-1 (alk. paper)
        1. Meditations. 2. Unitarian Universalist churches—Prayer-
     books and devotions—English. I. Frevert, Patricia. II. Collected
     meditations ; v. 3.

BX9855 .A44 2002
242—dc21   2002021157

5 4 3 2 1
04 03 02

The selections included here were previously published by Skinner House Books as follows: *Noisy Stones*, Robert R. Walsh, 1992; *In the Simple Morning Light*, Barbara Rohde, 1994; *Green Mountain Spring and Other Leaps of Faith*, Gary A. Kowalski, 1997; and *The Rock of Ages at the Taj Mahal*, Meg Barnhouse, 1999.

TABLE OF CONTENTS

FREEWHEELING

A TIME FOR DARKNESS

THE ONE TRUTH

AND THE RIVER FLOWS ON

"In the beginning was the word." This familiar introduction to John's gospel, intoned every Sunday in the church of my childhood, fairly captures my own experience as a child. Words are among my earliest memories, and some of the ones I remember best are from the stories, songs, rhymes, and prayers that were repeated over and over at home and at school.

In her book *Tender Mercies,* Anne Lamott says that the two best prayers are "please, please, please" and "thank you, thank you, thank you." Many of the meditations in this collection fall into this simple dyad of emotion—*oh yes,* and *oh no.* Uttered to a metaphorical god or to someone we experience as near and quite real, the prayer itself is holy and lively speech, from the top and the bottom of our hearts. Our prayers run the gamut of our feelings, from shame and guilt, to regret and grief, to gratitude and hopefulness.

Originally published as annual meditation manuals, these meditations are part of a cherished publishing ritual that has been observed by the Unitarian Universalist Association for more than forty years. Rooted in the annual lenten manual, today the tradition features authors from the laity as well as the ministry.

These prayers and reflections, artifacts in our hands, await our use. Alone or in company, whether we want to enter a mood of exuberant celebration, introduce a journey of fantasy, or initiate an atmosphere of loving gratitude, these words are for all this and more.

PATRICIA FREVERT

FOR ALL THE GIFTS OF LIFE

FOR ALL THE GIFTS OF LIFE

One summer morning—the morning of our forty-fifth wedding anniversary—we were awakened by the sound of two hummingbirds hovering among the feathery pink blossoms of the silk tree outside our bedroom window.

It was a small sound, more clicks than notes. It had none of the calling beauty of a cardinal's song, for example. And yet we experienced it as a gift, something life offered us for our particular delight.

Any event, when it nourishes our spirits, delights us, brings us energy or vision or direction or courage, is experienced as a gift. It is the genesis of all songs of praise.

Despite objective knowledge, we experience the sense of a gift as highly personal. I know, for example, that Channing did not write his sermon on spiritual freedom hoping that some day in the future someone like me would read it and see more clearly, but when a sentence from the sermon leaps off the page at me, I feel I have been directly addressed. Time has vanished and Channing is speaking his truth into my ear.

In our time it is difficult not to feel guilty about life's gifts, knowing that there are millions for whom a handful of rice would be the most important gift they could receive, knowing that millions are awakened by the sound of guns rather than by two hummingbirds in a silk tree.

A great temptation for the privileged is to ease our guilt by convincing ourselves that we have earned our gifts, by hard work or good deeds or the right creed. Or we go to the other extreme and adopt a kind of spiritual austerity program.

I believe such guilt is fruitless. Our task is to remember three things: gifts that are not received die; gifts that we try to hoard die; gifts that we cannot or do not hand to another die.

BARBARA ROHDE

FIRST SABBATH

Recently I reread the story of the first Sabbath, trying to approach it with the freshness of a seven-year-old mind, as I might have first read about Dr. Doolittle or the Wizard of Oz. In my seven-year-old persona, my first question was this: "What did God do on the Sabbath?" For those of us growing up in traditional religions, the talk was about what we shouldn't do. We shouldn't play cards. We shouldn't go to movies. We were told what we should stay away from, not what we should move toward.

Both the story and my own experience suggested that on that first Sabbath, along with resting, God was undoubtedly experiencing post-creation euphoria. Anyone who has written a story—or painted a picture, baked an elegant chocolate torte, built a house, made a quilt, or had a baby—can identify with God the creator. What has always delighted me is that after the second day and the third day and the fourth day, God looked at what he had done and saw that it was good, but after the sixth day he looked at all that he had done and saw that it was very good. It was only later that, like all other creators, he began to notice the flaws—the serpent beguiling Eve, Cain killing Abel. Indeed, by the sixth chapter of Genesis, God was repenting that he had ever started the whole thing. (Every creator can recognize this moment.)

But God spent the first Sabbath seeing the creation in all its harmony, blessing it and loving it. He needed to recognize and celebrate its value, which is the original meaning of worship.

I often forget that the first act of worship on the earth was God's worship of the creation, not the other way around.

BARBARA ROHDE

EARTH DAY

We give thanks for the earth and its creatures,
    and are grateful from A to Z:
For alligators, apricots, acorns, and apple trees,
For bumblebees, bananas, blueberries, and beagles,
Coconuts, crawdads, cornfields, and coffee,
Daisies, elephants, and flying fish,
For groundhogs, glaciers, and grasslands,
Hippos and hazelnuts, icicles and iguanas,
For juniper, jackrabbits, and junebugs,
Kudzu and kangaroos, lightning bugs and licorice,
For mountains and milkweed and mistletoe,
Norwhals and nasturtiums, otters and ocelots,
For peonies, persimmons, and polar bears,
Quahogs and Queen Anne's Lace,
For raspberries and roses,
Salmon and sassafras, tornadoes and tulipwood,
Urchins and valleys and waterfalls,
For X (the unknown, the mystery of it all!)
In every yak and yam;
We are grateful, good Earth, not least of all
For zinnias, zucchini, and zebras,
And for the alphabet of wonderful things
    that are as simple as ABC.

GARY A. KOWALSKI

BY ANY OTHER NAME

Physicists have the Big Bang theory. Hundreds of years ago, theologians developed a similar hypothesis called *creation ex nihilo*. This is the doctrine that the world sprang into being out of pure nothingness. One moment there was void and emptiness, and an instant later, quick as a divine heartbeat, a whole universe pulsed into view.

Now you see it, now you don't: That's Life. Trees that were absolutely barren a few days ago are now furred and fringed with a thousand shades of green. Everywhere, leaves seem to have materialized while I wasn't looking. An average apple tree (so I am told) has 100,000 of them. There may be a million on a single elm. One sugar maple has enough surface area on its foliage to cover over half an acre of ground (which I can well appreciate, having raked maple leaves from my front yard in the fall). Nature does nothing by half measures, but specializes in extravagance. All at once, and everywhere, creation happens.

If scientists ever want a new word to describe the initial singularity—the mysterious moment that brought it all into being—may I suggest some alternatives? How about the Big Budding? Or why not just call it Early Spring?

GARY A. KOWALSKI

"There is something you cannot find anywhere in the world," says a Hasidic proverb, "and yet there is, nevertheless, a place where you can find it."

The sacred cannot be restricted to any particular place or identified with any one person, yet it can be experienced as a dimension of depth present in all people and places. If you believe life's fulfillment lies elsewhere—in a higher income bracket, for instance, or a more austere ashram—you are chasing chimeras. Everything you need to be whole is already within reach. As we read in the prophets, "I am a God close at hand and not far off."

How close? Look inward to answer that question. Ask yourself: Am I living the life I was intended to live? Am I in tune with what is most authentic in myself? Do I know my own reason for being on this earth? As Rabbi Susya said shortly before his death, "In the world to come I will not be asked 'Why were you not Moses?' I shall be asked 'Why were you not Susya?'"

Another tale from the Hasidim: One day, after he had gone blind, Rabbi Bunam visited Rabbi Fishel, whose fame for miracle-cures had spread throughout the land. "Entrust yourself to my care," said his host. "I shall restore your sight."

"That is not necessary," said Bunam. "I see what I need to see."

May we too learn to see with the heart, and in the darkness that besets us within and without, discern the path that leads to life.

GARY A. KOWALSKI

CHRISTMAS EVE

Spirit of Christmas,
Spirit of Peace,
Spirit of Hope,
We gather in the depths of darkness
To bear witness to everlasting light;
Assembling at the turn of the year
To recall that which stands beyond time and change;
Joining with our families and loved ones
To acknowledge the brotherhood and sisterhood
That surpasses our singular loyalties
Uniting us as offspring of one Creation.
Into this sacred time we now enter
To listen, to dream, and to be transformed.
In this time of meditation,
May our thoughts be filled with gratitude and love:
Gratitude for our earth, shining in space, evergreen
     and radiant;
Gratitude for the enchantment of starlight
     And the infinite wonder of the night.

Gratitude for our children, and all children,
    The future of our world;
Love for life, the greatest of miracles;
Love for all those, far and near, who have blessed
our days
    With tenderness and affection
    And bestowed upon us memories of laughter
    and mirth.
Let us now be reconciled to this holy season.
Let us embrace this moment with joy.
Let the cares and worries of a hectic week
    Subside if only for an interval
    That our hearts might be touched with mystery
    and awe.
Silent as falling snow,
Effortless as descending night,
We rest now in quiet communion with our universe:
At one with holly bough and whispering pine.
Cradling all in love,
We sense our kinship with all people,
As the gentle glow of candlelight illumines our true
    features:
The grief and gladness written on each face
Giving dignity to every countenance.
We pray that the divinity within every creature
Might be made visible tonight
That every eye might see the world in newborn
    beauty

And that every voice might sing in praise.
We pray that compassion and goodwill
Might make their home with us,
Finding within our souls a welcome hearth
Burning brightly
With faith and hope and love.

GARY A. KOWALSKI

A COLLABORATIVE EFFORT

I have always lacked enthusiasm for Mother's Day
when I am the mother involved.

Birthdays are different. Birthdays are about who
I am inside, and what my history walking this earth
has been—what someone has called "the majesty of
particular existence." I'm pleased when people tell
me they're glad they have shared some of that life
with me and would like to share more. But I tend to
think of a Mother's Day celebration as a generic
birthday party.

I suppose my lukewarm feeling toward the day
began when my children were very young and each
year served me lukewarm eggs for a "surprise"
breakfast in bed. Sitting in solitary splendor with my
glass of skim milk rather than my usual steaming
coffee, I would much rather have been downstairs

with the rest of the family, giggling around the dining room table.

But the older I get, the stronger understanding grows of how many people have helped to create and to nourish my children's bodies and spirits. I feel silly being singled out for praise when I remember the gifted teachers who inspired them, the adult friends who comforted them, their comrades throughout the years who have loved them and challenged them and kept them singing.

If we're going to observe the day, let's recognize that as parents we did not raise our children by ourselves. Let us remember, as children, how many people it took to bring our being into existence.

Let us praise those who have created us and bequeathed to us the gifts of life. Let us praise our mother and our father for our genetic legacy and for the care they have given us.

But let us also praise those who have preserved and passed on our great cultural heritage. Let us praise those who have nourished us physically, but also those who have stimulated our minds and fed our spirits; those who have created a home for us, but those also who labor so long to make the world more homelike. As we praise these people, let us vow to hand down this legacy, not merely to our own children, but to all the children of the earth.

BARBARA ROHDE

MUD SEASON

People in northern New England understand why April is called the cruelest month. All the snow melts at once.

You can concentrate on the mud or focus on the puddles, and I prefer the latter. On the surface of the water, I can see reflections of sun, clouds, trees, and sky—a refracted mirror of heaven above. In the few inches of moisture at my feet, I realize that there are millions of tiny organisms swimming, feasting, breeding, and dying—a microscopic world teeming with life. And if the mathematicians who study fractals are right, the coastline of one average-sized puddle is long enough to stretch to the moon and back, pocketed with more miniscule inlets, bays, and backwaters than the outline of an entire continent. There is literally a cosmos at my feet with enough physics, biology, and geography to fill a lifetime with fascination.

Such thoughts soothe my mind when my socks are cold and wet. Although it's fine to give into my flights of fancy, I better keep my eyes firmly on the pavement during mud season in Vermont.

GARY A. KOWALSKI

EMPTINESS

My wife and I collect empty jars. Whenever we finish a jar of pickles, peanut butter, or what have you, we save it to fill with beans that we buy in bulk from the food co-op. Their varied sizes, shapes, and colors brighten up our kitchen counter: red kidneys, yellow peas, black beans, white navies, and green split peas, a lovely litany of legumes. Collecting jars gives us a goal to strive for; and because our goal is relatively modest, we have the satisfaction of attaining it. It's not an overarching or transcendent purpose, but sometimes simple, everyday actions create a little beauty and add a bit of meaningful pleasure to our lives. I may not know much about God or Absolutes or Truth with a capital "T," but at least I know beans.

GARY A. KOWALSKI

SURPRISED BY LOVE

A funeral director in a nearby town called to ask if I would do a graveside service. It was for a man named Melvin.

I interviewed Melvin's cousin on the phone. Melvin had worked in a landscaping business belonging to another cousin. He was good with the plants and the soil, but not very good with money or with people. His mother left him her house, and he lived there alone until it got to be such a mess that it was uninhabitable. Then a few years ago he moved to Leominster, where he lived with a family who owned a motel. He was their handy man and helped take care of their kids. "That was odd," the cousin said, "because my kids couldn't stand him."

I called a man who worked with Melvin. He told a similar story. "I don't know what you could say," he admitted. "There probably won't be many people there."

It seemed Melvin's life had been a problem. It sounded as if these people were just going through the motions of having a service.

I got out the usual text I use for such occasions. The opening words and the prayer spoke of a person who was loved, and of survivors mourning their loss. I thought, these words would not be true for these people. They would know that I was only reading stock lines.

So where I usually say, "We have come here because someone we knew and loved has died; we are forever less because he has gone," I substituted, "We have come here because someone we knew has died."

And where I usually say, "We rejoice in his life and give thanks that we have walked the way with such a companion," I substituted, "We give thanks for his life."

There were about a dozen people at the grave site. I was asked to wait for some latecomers. At ten minutes past the hour a car pulled up. A woman and two teenagers got out. When the funeral director motioned the people to gather near the grave, the latecomers stood in front of the others.

As I began my laundered remarks the three of them started to weep. Large tears rolled down. They sobbed.

When it was over I spoke to one of the red-eyed teenagers. This was the family from Leominster. She told me how Melvin had lived in their house and cared for them, and then how the roles reversed. She told of his long illness, how she had taken food and medicine to his room when he was in pain and could barely swallow. And she told me of the day she had found him dead. She loved him. She began to cry again.

None of the people knew about the words I did not say. Several of them thanked me for the service, and I believe all of them were satisfied with it. But I was not satisfied. I was taken by surprise. I had prepared myself to meet indifference, but love showed up instead.

I am going to try never again to assume that any person is not loved. I am going to try to prepare for love.

Maybe today I will notice a spark of love in someone's heart. Maybe this time I will not be surprised.

ROBERT R. WALSH

THESE STONES DO NOT LACK INTEREST

These stones do not lack interest even though
their passive presence on the dresser top
awaits initiative from me. They go
for weeks without the least attention.

These stones have pleasing rounded shapes,
their quiet colors uniform or varied.
Some have faded stripes or circles, some
are spotted. Some are intersected by
contrasting seams of other kinds of rock.
One white stone has a cross of black. And one
looks like a cream cheese sandwich.

These stones have got integrity. They rest
in dryness of the air, on smoothness of
the wood, in incandescent light, presenting
grainy surfaces that are exactly
what they seem to be.
                           The stones
I picked up weren't like this.

Motions of the tides had brought them to
the great margin of earth and sea and sky.
The stones I chose from all the others showed
me surfaces that shone with cold fire.

I was the passive one. Each one of these
commanded me to pause. The colors came

as if from deep within: the shining yellows,
glowing ochres, whites as pure as any
pearl, the rings like bands of Jupiter,
the blacks as black as space between the stars.

And now they rest, in isolation, dusty,
far removed from forces that gave them
their form. I have interrupted for
a while their evolution toward becoming
sand grains.
        But I remember when
I plucked them from the great margin. I
remember seeing them in moving noisy
bright abrasive wetness. How they shone!

ROBERT R. WALSH

SUMMER READING

Great Author of Creation
Whose brilliance is written
On the page of every day,
Who has given us the book of nature
In which to read
The glory of our birth,
Whose handwriting is in the stars,
And whose manuscript fills the earth:
We give thanks for the energies of the spirit

That sing forth your praise,
For poets and makers of rhymes,
For storytellers and spellbinders,
For writers comic and tragic
Who enlarge our imaginations and elevate our minds.
We give thanks for great literature
And the revelations of every scripture:
For thinkers and philosophers,
Prophets and wizards,
Myth-makers and oracles
Who lift up our wonder
And deepen our acquaintance with mystery.
We give thanks for every style and genre
That speaks to our condition:
For humor, for romance, for drama,
And for words that touch the heights and
    depths of being.
But in this season of leisure, we are especially grateful
For thrillers, potboilers, and pageturners,
Junk food for the brain,
Which does nothing to nourish our souls
But always leaves us hungry for more.
O, let us never grow tired of reading
Or of the refreshment it brings.
And let us be glad that of the making of books
There is no end.

GARY A. KOWALSKI

GIVING THANKS

My grandfather often told the story of a cowboy who had just lassoed a steer with a lariat tied to his horse's saddle. Suddenly he noticed a big tree in front of him, and the horse and the steer were headed for opposite sides of it. Figuring it was time to say his prayers, the cowboy recited the only one he knew: "Lord, make us grateful for these blessings we are about to receive."

Like the fictional cowboy, many of us are at a loss when we need a prayer for that special occasion. Here is one you may want to share with your families this Thanksgiving:

Loving Spirit,
Be our guest,
Dine with us,
Share our bread,
That our table
Might be blessed
And our souls be fed.

A prayer can be spoken or silent. It need not be addressed to any deity we know or can name. What it should do is express our sense of joyful participation with the gracious forces of life. If you don't like mine, say a prayer of your own, or use the old cowboy's. The important thing is to give thanks.

For all the bumps and bruises along the way, it remains a heckuva ride.

GARY A. KOWALSKI

POP'S PRAYER

My earliest memory of a prayer is the table grace my grandfather used to say. I associate it with holiday meals, with extended family crowded around a long dining room table. I remember the smell of turkey gravy, the sight of bowed heads—and then the gruff voice of this old man delivering the prayer as if it were one long word accented on the first and last syllables: "*Lord*makeusthankfulfortheseprovisionswe-askinchristsake*amen.*"

The last word sounded like "gah-*men!*" I thought that was the way one ended a prayer.

I remember years when I had no idea what he was saying. The prayer had meaning that did not depend on knowing. It was an invocation for the larger liturgy of the meal. Its meanings, beyond language, had to do with bonds: my bonds to the food, my parents and sister, the aunts and uncles and cousins and grandparents there, the warmth of the room, the celestial and human rhythms that brought us to that table, and other mysteries beyond these.

There came a time when I figured out the words to Pop's prayer, but that did not seem to affect its meaning. It was much, much later, after turning this memory over until it was worn smooth, that I realized something important about the prayer. I had thought it was a prayer of thanksgiving. But Pop did not say, "Lord, thank you." He said, "Lord, make us thankful." It was a prayer of petition.

We were beginning those special meals, not with thanks for the bountiful gifts before us and around us, but with a confession that we were not thankful enough. "Make us thankful." Wake us up. Our gratitude is dulled by the very abundance of what we have. Bring us, somehow, to enough clarity of vision to see what a miracle is this creation in which we find ourselves.

In truth, we are not thankful enough: a confession with which to begin our thanksgiving. Gah-*men*!

ROBERT R. WALSH

FREEWHEELING

FREEWHEELING

When I was young, my friends and I used to take "penny hikes." We would head down the street on foot or bike to the closest intersection, then flip a coin. Heads we would go right, tails to the left. At the next corner, we would repeat the process. Of course, if there was someplace we really wanted to go, like the drug store to look at comics, we could always cheat a little, but there was something exciting about sauntering through the world without any fixed destination in mind. The element of chance transformed our sleepy, suburban neighborhood into *terra incognita*. Where would we end? What surprises might surface along the way?

I still like to hike and bike to nowhere in particular. I travel farther now than I did then, but it's not the distance nor the novelty of new surroundings that creates the allure (Vermont doesn't get all that exotic). It's knowing that life, which is sometimes predictable, can still contain odd turns and open vistas. Wherever you happen to be is the center of a circle that radiates in all directions.

Take a chance . . . invite the unexpected. You may get lost, but you can never get bored. The best part is that after all these years, a penny will still take you as far as you want to go.

GARY A. KOWALSKI

I know beauty and grace are all around me. Sometimes I know how to be there for it. Other times I get distracted by my bank balance dipping into the negative, by my child coughing, by my body aging, or by someone somewhere being disappointed in me.

Usually it is clear to me that I have the choice to stew about things or to be there for my life. In her book *The Intuitive Body,* Aikido Master Wendy Palmer writes that you get what you pay for when it comes to your attention. Whatever you pay attention to, that is what you get. If you pay attention to the things that are nuisances, your life feels like one big nuisance. If you pay attention to beauty and joy, then your life fills up with beauty and joy.

Last weekend I was paying attention to ninety-degree heat and shoving crowds, standing in line for the bumper car ride with my two boys. One of them kept changing his mind about the ride. What he really wanted to do was toss rubber chickens into a small pot, five tries for two dollars. My brain was a rubber chicken.

I had just dragged the children all over the fair, looking for the writers with whom I was supposed to sign books. I was also looking for the folks from my congregation who were selling beer. I couldn't find either group and the whole time I was looking, both boys were pulling on me and asking, "Can we ride the rides now?" I didn't even have the energy to start the "do you know the difference between 'can' and 'may'?" discussion since my nine year old last time said, "Yeah, mom. 'May' is a month and 'can' is a tin container." Sigh. So I said, "Let's go ride the rides," and here we were in line and into my head came this thought: "I am in hell."

Once I saw my older son dive into a car and start twirling the wheel, waiting for the ride to start, I moved into the shade with his brother to watch. There my brain cooled off enough to remember to enjoy my life, to be there for the beauty and grace in that situation. I saw my son's mouth open wide with joy, its inside stained red by a tiger's blood-flavored shaved ice.

He was in bliss, being slammed from behind and from all sides by other bumper car drivers. He threw back his head and laughed, putting the pedal to the metal in reverse, snapping his head forward as he took aim and slammed into another car, looking sideways at the other driver, grinning, not quite able to believe this was actually allowed.

Jubilee. Bubbles of joy changed my breathing. I was having fun. Here was beauty and here was grace and here I was in the middle of it. Jubilee indeed.

MEG BARNHOUSE

THE PUZZLING WARMTH OF CHAOS

Visiting my son and his family one November, I awakened the first morning to the wonderful sounds of a house coming to life, to that once-familiar chaos of getting off to school, the sounds of small feet in the hallway, flushings and brushings, showerings and scourings, and the occasional loud whisper, "Shhh! Grandma's still asleep."

When I hear the last of the feet going down the stairs to breakfast, I venture into the bathroom, push aside the large collection of boats, pails, frogs, ducks, and fish in the bottom of the tub, and take my shower. Putting on my warmest sweater and my old wool slacks, I go down to greet them, to have my communal bowl of Cheerios, and to help in the final search for the missing jacket, the hidden shoe, the perfect thing for Show and Tell before they hurry out to the road to catch the schoolbus. Then I pour myself a cup of coffee and sit down with the mildly exhausted Mom and Dad to enjoy the sudden splendid silence of the morning.

I am swept by a wave of nostalgia that surprises me. I have become so fond of the solitude of early morning that it seems strange to find that part of me misses the chaos. I realize that I probably no longer have the agile energy that would allow me to wander safely through that chaos for very long. Still, in the midst of the final movement of life's symphony, I miss the scherzo.

I suppose that is why I sometimes go to both services on Christmas Eve—the one in which the toddlers wander in the aisles, babies sometimes cry, and the beginning violinists join the motley orchestra that accompanies the carols; the one in quiet candlelight, where one can hear every note of the skilled musicians, every word of the poet's wisdom, where one can even sit in moments of rich silence and reflect on the meaning of the season.

Scientists studying the growth and uniqueness of snowflakes have found two things: the laws of pattern formation are universal and the final flake records the history of all the changing weather conditions it has experienced. Perhaps this represents a religious truth as well as a scientific one. In solitude we intuit the intended pattern of human growth (what once was called "the voice of God"). In experiencing the turbulent weather of life and responding to it, we become our own unique selves.

BARBARA ROHDE

SUBVERSIVE BEHAVIOR

When I was teaching a class called "Women in Religion," I gave my students an assignment. For the duration of the class we were going to talk about God as "she" and "Mother" instead of "he" and "Father." I know it's ridiculous to call God "she," as if God were female. But it's equally ridiculous to call God "he," as if God were male. Since the Judeo-Christian culture has been calling God "he" for the last four thousand years, I told my students, perhaps one semester of calling God "she" will begin to balance that a bit. Every semester their reactions were explosive. One young woman said angrily, "I could *never* call on a mother God if I really needed help. She wouldn't have the power to do anything." What does that say about her sense of her own mother? About her sense of herself as a female?

Another student had gone out to dinner with her parents and was telling them about our class and about having to call God "Mother." A waitress hovered behind them, wiping a table for long minutes and listening. When they got up to leave, she came over to my student and said, "Honey, you better quit calling God 'Mother' because if you don't, you're goin' straight to hell."

I usually keep my efforts at education confined to the classroom, but not always. I was scheduled to

speak to a women's group at a small country church
several years ago, and when I arrived nothing was
ready, no one was gathered. I'm not even sure the
minister had told anyone I was coming. I was left on
my own in the Sunday school wing of the building
while they got themselves organized. I wandered
into the nursery and then into what looked like a
primary grade classroom. There were crayons and
blunt scissors, scraps of colored paper on low tables.
On a bulletin board, I saw a picture in crayon on
pink construction paper of a man with wings, a halo,
a long brown beard, and a serious expression. The
caption, in large capital letters, read "GOD."

What else could I do? I looked around for more
construction paper and, with a crayon, I drew a
picture of a woman with a smile, gray curly hair, and
big breasts. I gave her wings and a halo and wrote in
big letters the caption: "GOD."

When people hear about the Supreme Being as
being only male, they get unbalanced. If God is
male, then males are closer to what God is like than
females. Men might start to feel like they are supposed to know everything and be able to control
everything, like they can't stop and ask for directions when they need to. How exhausting.

Women might start to feel like their bodies and
spirits are less sacred than men's, like their ways of
doing things are wrong or stupid and that God

doesn't care much about birthing or bleeding or feeding a child from their body. They might start to doubt whether they know anything or can control anything. That's exhausting, too.

As a therapist, I have seen the results of this exhaustion and imbalance. That's why I do my little part to drive people nuts. Because where people are going nuts, you know something important is going on.

MEG BARNHOUSE

ROCK OF AGES AT THE TAJ MAHAL

In July of 1985 I was on a bus in the middle of India with forty Muslims, Hindus, Jews, Christians, Buddhists, and Moonies. We were touring the world for two months to study each others' religions.

We were on our way to the Taj Mahal, four hours from our hotel in New Delhi. The bus was painted turquoise to ward off evil spirits and hung all over with garlands of marigolds. The day was hot; the road was dusty and full of holes. I was sitting next to Gary from Alabama, who had been raised Southern Baptist but was now a Moonie, and we talked as the bus bumped and jolted us down the road.

I love talking to people who are on the fringes of my religious experience. Hearing about exotic beliefs and strange practices is one of my favorite hobbies. The Moonies certainly seemed out there on the fringe to me, so I had been pestering them to tell me what they believed. We had a good time questioning each other, sometimes debating, often laughing. Gary and I had gotten to be friends. One of the things we all did to pass the time on long bus rides was to look through each other's wallets, perusing pictures of loved ones, mocking driver's license photos, flipping through insurance cards, love notes, and bank receipts.

Another thing we did to pass the time on long bus and plane rides was to tell what we'd be doing this day and this hour if we were home. It was a Saturday, and I was telling Gary that my husband and I would be getting ready to go over to our friends' house for supper. We would grill chicken, eat vegetables with spinach dip, and sit in the dining room under the black velvet painting of Elvis. The painting had been an anniversary gift from us, and they would hang it up on Saturday nights when we came over. After supper we would move to the living room and sing hymns around the piano, starting with the Navy Hymn about "those in peril on the sea," working up to what we called "blood hymns." Blood hymns were the old timey ones about the blood of Jesus, the ones with the questionable theology and stirring tunes that so many of us secretly love.

Gary said, "I know about blood hymns—I grew up Southern Baptist!" We started singing. We harmonized on "There's Power in the Blood" and "There is a Fountain Filled With Blood" and "Are You Washed in the Blood?" We had a fine time, and we got applause from the Sikhs who were sitting behind us with their long beards, white turbans, and curved daggers on their belts. They sang us some Sikh songs and we applauded. Then the Buddhist monks from Nepal sitting across the aisle were moved to chant, and the sound of their voices resonated through the turquoise bus, making our breastbones vibrate. That hot afternoon for hours we heard Russian Orthodox hymns, songs from Finland, Rasta gospel from Jamaica, and a spell for making yourself impervious to fire from a witch doctor named André who lives in Surinam with his ten beautiful wives and forty-seven children.

These days, when I hear about the peaceable kingdom where the lion will lie down with the lamb, when I read about the clamor of nations struggling toward peace, I think about that day we sang our spirituals for each other, the day when Christ and Shiva clapped for each other and sang in harmony on a dusty road in a turquoise bus hung with marigolds.

MEG BARNHOUSE

FOURTH OF JULY

"Give me your tired, your poor, your huddled masses
yearning to breathe free."
—EMMA LAZARUS (INSCRIBED ON THE STATUE OF LIBERTY)

Over a century ago, Wilhelm Kosanke arrived in New
York City with twenty-five cents in his pocket and a
train ticket to Kansas. He was only twelve years old.

Will had planned to make the journey with his
older brother to join an uncle who was already
settled in the new land. The two of them were
boarding the gangplank of the steamer that would
take them across the Atlantic when the Kaiser's
military police seized his brother to conscript him in
the army. Will boarded alone. Fortunately, he was
able to find a German-speaking policeman in
Manhattan, who helped him locate the train station.
"Wo ist Kansas, bitte? Können Sie mir helfen?" How
confusing the babble of languages must have been!
With his last two-bits, he bought a loaf of bread and
a piece of sausage to last him on the four-day ride to
find his relatives. I know, because Wilhelm Kosanke
was my great-grandfather.

Now the saga continues. Where else but in this
multiracial, multilingual, multicultural mélange
would you find a Korean child named Gary A.
Kowalski? His place of birth was near Nonsan,
and his family heritage is Asian, as well as Welsh,

German, and Polish. But like the rest of us, my son
is indubitably American . . .

> as American as pizza,
> or eggrolls,
> or tacos,
> or apple pie,
> or would you believe *kielbasa* and *kimchi* to go?

GARY A. KOWALSKI

FIREWORKS AT THE WEDDING

I dreamed one night that fireworks had exploded
and blown a big hole in the church where I grew up.
Fireworks and church may not seem to go together,
but in my family they do.

In the North Carolina branch of my mother's
family, we have fireworks at every major celebration:
the Fourth of July, New Year's, Thanksgiving, Christmas, birthdays, the first and last days of school, and
weddings. Especially weddings. This is in all other
ways a dignified and conservative family, filled with
doctors and ministers, teachers, lawyers, and mis-
sionaries. It was my missionary grandfather who
brought the custom back from India where fireworks enliven the best festivities. Several of the
dignified pillars of the family disapprove of fireworks

at weddings, so we have to sneak to set them off. Fireworks aren't the only mischief in the family, but they are the central mischief.

At a recent family wedding, I heard one of my cousins talking to his two-year-old nephew. "Darlin'," he said, "there is going to be a beautiful lady in that church carrying some flowers. Now, son, some of those flowers are for you. So when she walks by, you just run up and grab you a handful . . ."

As the service began, one cousin slipped outside. No one noticed. We practice not noticing; it's part of the protocol. A few minutes later, when my opera singer cousin was hitting the high notes in "Where Sheep May Safely Graze," we heard the cannon fire. Then, from right outside the open windows came the rapid-fire volleys of the Black Cats that come in strings of twenty or thirty firecrackers. It made an ungodly racket. The entire crowd on the groom's side of the church jumped in their seats and looked around, wild-eyed. The cellist in the string quartet fell off her chair. On the bride's side, my family gazed calmly straight ahead, squinting a little against the acrid smoke that drifted through the windows into the sanctuary. No one giggled. That is against the code. No one even smiled.

At one family wedding, the minister was told by the mother of the bride about our tradition of fireworks. She did not want any fireworks at this wedding. Like we say here in the South, that minister had a fit and fell in it. He instructed the rehearsal party on the sacredness of the occasion, a sacredness that was not to be sullied by fun or high spirits. To drive his point home, he told the Old Testament story about two people who touched the Ark of the Covenant without permission. They were struck dead for sullying a sacred thing. The wedding party stared at their shoes. This wasn't covered in our family wedding protocol.

At this wedding, guards were hired and posted outside the church building. One string of Black Cats did get lit, but we only heard three pops.Those strings are hard to stop once they get started. I imagine one of the guards threw himself bodily on it. There was a brief incident at the reception where an uncle set off his cannon and his sister, the mother of the bride, called the police. They came and investigated. There was a lot of talking into police radios, but, in Kings Mountain, North Carolina, the police just don't arrest orthopedic surgeons in the middle of the day, even if they shoot off a fireworks cannon in a residential area.

My dream was telling me a truth. Fireworks did blow a hole in that childhood church of mine. Each explosion let in a little fresh air. They supply a welcome balance to the self-sacrifice and stern structure that is so much a part of that religious tradition. I left that church long ago for a freer and more liberal one, but I honor joy and celebration in any religion. I'm glad to have been taught that the sacred and the silly walk well hand in hand.

MEG BARNHOUSE

WE THREE KINGS AND FOURTEEN SCHIZOPHRENICS

All I can say is you haven't lived until you've sung "We Three Kings" with fourteen paranoid schizophrenics on Christmas Eve.

At seven o'clock the Christmas Eve I was fifteen, my father developed an urgent need to go caroling. He loved the idea of serving humanity, but the actuality of serving humanity was too time-consuming, too much trouble, and too little applauded for any of us to have done much of it. Christmas is a time, though, when one's thoughts turn to helping others. You watch "A Christmas Carol" and "It's a Wonderful Life" and you feel moved to do something loving and giving.

My dad had not yet done any Christmas service to humanity, and since it was Christmas Eve, the deadline was fast approaching. We hadn't even bought our Christmas tree, but my dad had an impulse to go caroling, and he wanted me and my thirteen-year-old sister to go with him.

We wailed that it would be terminally embarrassing to go caroling with him around our neighborhood. The neighborhood, he informed us cheerfully, was not what he had in mind. He felt called to go caroling eight miles down the road—at the Norristown State Mental Hospital.

If you have ever known a teenage girl, you know my sister and I had sulking, sighing, and rolling our eyes raised to an art form. My dad, though, was an artist himself: at growling, jollying, guilting, and flashing a charismatic personality. By seven-thirty we were slumped in the back seat of the blue Olds. My twelve-string guitar was riding in the trunk. By seven forty-five we pulled up to the heavy wrought-iron gates of the mental hospital.

My dad had called ahead and spoken to someone in the office, but that person had not told the guards at the gate. At first they looked at us with suspicion, but my father was famous in Philadelphia at that time because he was on the 6 and 11 o'clock TV news. They had seen his face before. In five minutes they had been charmed into believing we weren't there to break out an insane serial killer, so they let us in and gave us directions to the building where they thought we might want to sing.

The staff people in that building were surprised to see us, too, but they were kind. With good grace they began directing patients to the lobby where we three carolers stood. The staff set up chairs while we waited.

I was completely humiliated. I let my hair hang in front of my face and pretended to be invisible. My little sister copied me, naturally. The patients started shuffling in, holding their heads at a too-far-back angle that I now know meant heavy doses of Thorazine.
In their dishwater gray hospital gowns it was hard to tell anyone's age. Everybody looked old, even the young ones. They shuffled to their chairs. My dad motioned for me to get out my guitar.

We started with "The First Noel" and "Hark! The Herald Angels Sing." A woman wearing bright red lipstick on her lips, her cheekbones, and in a circle on her chin, slapped her legs and sang loudly in time with the music. Her voice sounded like something between a crow and a warning siren, and she didn't bother with words. She especially liked "Joyful, Joyful, We Adore Thee." We started smiling at each other. Her enjoyment became a blaze that caught in the rest of us. One by one, each of the patients joined us in singing. It was during "We Three Kings" that I forgot to act cool. We were having Christmas, and the whole dark place, just for a moment, was lit with joy.

MEG BARNHOUSE

LAUNDROMAT OUTLAW

I broke the rules at the laundromat. I plead ignorance. For most of my life I have been rich and I didn't know it. I have lived with a washer and dryer right in the same house with me. My new house didn't have either appliance, so for the first week I took my clothes to the Clean 1 Washeteria.

It looks the same as the laundromat I used at school in New Jersey. It looks the same as the one I used to go to with my mother when I was nine in Statesville, North Carolina. There are rows of washing machines, rows of dryers, a woman supervising the room, and a blaring TV. People sit on plastic chairs reading or watching soap operas while their laundry washes and dries.

I have a problem with sitting. I'm recently divorced and still in that attention-deficit stage where I can't focus on anything for longer than fifteen minutes. I could no more sit and watch TV while my clothes washed than climb Mount Everest.

I put my clothes in their washers and left. When I got back the clothes were done. I had been gone so long I was surprised my clothes were still in the washers. I expected them to be in wet heaps on one of the counters. I put everything in two dryers and left again. When I got back after a couple of hours, the supervisor was waiting for me, leaning on her mop and looking stern. She said my clothes had been sitting in those dryers for an hour and people were waiting to use the machines and I really should be more consistent. (I think she meant "considerate.") I was horrified. I am never inconsiderate. Well, only when I'm driving. When not under the influence of asphalt, I'm a wonderful person.

If someone needed the dryer and my clothes were finished, why didn't they just take my clothes out and leave them piled on a counter? The laundromat I remember in New Jersey had piles of wet clothes on the counters, piles of dry clothes in rolling baskets. No one had to sit around stewing because somebody's clothes were finished and they weren't back to get them. The clothes would have been wrinkled, but wrinkles were the price you paid for freedom. The culture of this laundromat is different. The women sat, needing to do their wash, not willing to move my clothes. And I had to stand there and be scolded by the laundry lady.

I hate being scolded. It takes me back to third grade, and that was not a good year. I stuffed my dry clothes in bags and slunk away, a laundromat outlaw. I hate breaking rules by accident, so I conducted a completely unscientific poll on the Law of the Laundromat. I asked a number of people to pretend someone else's wash was finished and sitting in the machine. Would they take out the wash and leave the person's wet clothes on the counter? Would they take dry clothes out of a dryer and leave them in one of those rolling wire baskets? At first the responses were divided along the Mason-Dixon line, with Southerners represented by my best friend, who says you don't mess with other people's messes.

Another Southern friend said nonsense, she'd have taken my clothes out and dumped them on the counter in a skinny minute if she needed the machine. She is a first-grade teacher, and they know how to take charge of an unruly world.

Maybe it's politeness that kept those women waiting for the machines occupied by my laundry. Maybe it was passivity. I can't tell. Sometimes politeness and passivity look the same to me. I would prefer not to stomp around stewing, waiting for other people to do what I think is the right thing. I don't want them to stomp around waiting for me to do what they think is the right thing, either. They would probably have a long wait.

I am going to try to figure out what the right thing is at this laundromat before I go back. That supervisor lady is someone I don't want to cross again. Meanwhile, these days I have a washer and dryer at my house. I'm going to go kiss them now.

MEG BARNHOUSE

PRISONER OF COOL

I had a crisis of coolness while standing in line at the post office. I was waiting to mail a package, minding my own business, when I heard a bird in the room. A big bird, tweeting and chirping, sounding like it was coming from the ceiling.

Here's where my mind started tripping over itself. If some human being were making that sound, it would be uncool to look around, craning my neck to see the birds in the ceiling. That person would be chirping to make me look for the bird, so they could be amused at how gullible and goofy I was.

On the other hand, I refuse to be a fearful person. I don't want to turn into someone who can stand in line right under a huge chirping bird and not even glance around for fear of looking like an idiot. That would make me a prisoner of cool.

I have known prisoners of cool. They can't have much fun. They don't let themselves laugh loudly in the movies; they can't be thrilled by a beautiful sight or delighted by an ordinary moment. They're always saying things like: "Take it easy . . ." or "You're easy to please . . ." when they deign to speak. Usually the ones I know just give sardonic looks from under a raised eyebrow, or they shake their heads with a secret smile.

A prisoner of cool would never crane her neck in the post office to look for a big bird. In making the decision to look or not to look, which took about ten seconds in actual post office time, I asked myself two questions: "What do you want to do?" and "What would the woman you want to become do?"

I want to become the kind of woman who has such amazing powers that she can know not only which of the people standing in line behind her was making a bird noise, but also the thoughts of each person there, along with what was in their hearts. I want to be able to sense the vibrations of whatever life forms were in the building and be able to communicate with them telepathically.

I didn't have the feeling that my amazing powers were going to kick in that day. Even if they never do, I want to become a great old person. You know how some old people seem to have a deep affection for the dailiness of life, and others are always dissatisfied and disappointed? I have a friend whose mother says every year, "This year's fall colors just aren't as brilliant as last year's." She has said that for the past twenty years. Are the leaves growing dull or are her senses?

I want to become an old woman who would crane her neck looking for the bird. So that's what I did. There wasn't a bird. The man behind the desk noticed me looking around and said in a bored voice, "That guy comes in here and does that all the time."

In back of me was a round man with slick black hair who looked energetically innocent. The bird-call man. He was good. I felt dumb, which annoyed me. What a geeky joke.

That's just my youth talking, though. The old woman I am going to become would throw her head back and laugh. She might compliment the man on his bird-call prowess. Maybe even ask for a lesson. Now that's a cool old lady.

MEG BARNHOUSE

STOP, LOOK, AND LISTEN

Have you noticed that more and more cars are running red lights? I have. Apparently a yellow light no longer means "slow down," but in the minds of many drivers means "put the pedal to the metal." Maybe it is symptomatic of people in our society, who seem in an ever greater hurry to get to the front of the line, regardless of who they might run over in the process.

It is the little things that count, and small infractions like these do add up. I am reminded of a story (possibly true) in which several international business executives were crossing a busy street in downtown Tokyo. Because the coast was clear, the

Americans in the group didn't bother to wait for the walk sign and forged across the avenue. When their Japanese companions joined them after the walk sign had given the go ahead, the Westerners were puzzled. "Why didn't you cross with us?" they asked. "You could see there were no cars coming."

"True," the Japanese replied, looking upward toward the tall buildings all around, "but a small child might have been watching from one of those windows. And if we had crossed against the light, what would that little one have learned?"

I am consciously trying to slow down these days, thinking of that young child. I will paste it on my mental refrigerator door, if not on the bumper of my car: "I brake for pedestrians and stop signs (not to mention animals, bicycles, and traffic cops)." Certainly, if we all gave as much thought to how we get somewhere as to how fast we arrive, the world would be a better place.

GARY A. KOWALSKI

THE FOSSIL RECORD

A year ends leaving me to wonder what I have to show for it. While I don't have a quick answer, I do derive some consolation from natural history.

I think of how fossils are formed. Only "hard parts" are preserved in geological strata, with very rare exceptions. Skeletons, teeth, shells, and carapaces, covered with sediment, may slowly turn to rock and last for millions of years. But the living interior of an organism—its nerves and muscles, its flesh and spirit—disappear and leave no trace. Everything that makes life interesting is evanescent. Although paleontologists may claim to teach us the history of life, all they can really offer is a chronicle of the lifeless features that once vital beings left behind.

That is probably how I feel. I may have acquired some hard information and definite insights that will become part of my personal fossil record—proof that some kind of intellectual or spiritual evolution has taken place these past twelve months—but these bits of evidence are like trilobites or crinoids, once living, but now merely lingering impressions clinging to the surface of things. Whatever has the capacity to move and grow and stir the soul will remain unobserved and ineffable.

Another year has ended (as so much in life ends) with not much solid to show for it. But solidity is for dry bones and other desiccated remnants. That, I hope, is one of the main differences between fossils and me.

GARY A. KOWALSKI

49

WARNING FROM THE STEAMSHIP AUTHORITY

I emptied my pockets at the end of the day and found among the coins and keys a small piece of paper that read: "NOT VALID IF DETACHED." It was a stub from a ferry boat ticket.

Not valid if detached. Is it true? Maybe not. Detachment can be valuable. Sometimes it is important to get a detached view. A person who is detached, and therefore objective, is a more reliable witness in a court of law. A juror might say, "Not valid *unless* detached."

It is possible to become so attached to a person or a cause that we cannot distinguish our own issues from those of another. In such a relationship we may not take care of ourselves. A measure of detachment under such circumstances can be healing for all concerned. We might even say, "*More* valid if *more* detached."

Still, I want to listen to the warning on the ticket stub, for being detached can also mean being indifferent. Being objective about another person may make it possible to treat that person as an object. Being detached from the world or any of its parts can make it easier for us to avoid our responsibility for it.

To strike a member of our family we must first be detached. To permit our teenage children to have unchaperoned drinking parties in our homes we must be detached. We must be detached if we are to paint a swastika on a synagogue, tell a disparaging joke about gay people, cut public health care and nutrition programs for poor children, or drop bombs on a civilian neighborhood in Panama City.

It is only through our detachment that we are able to rend the ozone layer, poison the air and the sea, exterminate whole species of animals, and burn the rain forests.

There are times when some detachment is appropriate and necessary. But the greatest source of evil in our time may be that we are too detached from people, and too detached from the earth. If we meet everything objectively, then there is no sacredness and no mystery.

Listen to the warning.

ROBERT R. WALSH

A TIME FOR DARKNESS

"In the bleak midwinter frosty wind made moan, earth stood hard as iron, water like stone. Snow had fallen, snow on snow, snow on snow, in the bleak midwinter long ago."

This is the season when dark is growing strong, reaching its peak at the winter solstice on December 21. On December 22, the earth begins tilting the Northern Hemisphere gradually back toward our sun. The light begins to grow stronger, and every culture in the Northern Hemisphere celebrates the rebirth of the light. Hindus have Divali, Jews have Hannukah, Pagans have Yule, Christians have Christmas.

Jesus was probably born in spring, since the story says shepherds were out in the fields at night, and it is usually too cold for that in Bethlehem at the end of December. The Christian Church set the date of Jesus' birth celebration to coincide with a huge celebration in the Roman Empire that was already taking place on December 25. That way the birth of the Son could be celebrated at the same time as the birth of the Sun. Both are symbols of the birth of The Light in the hearts and minds of human beings.

For some of us, The Light as a symbol can represent the light of reason, by which we find our way in life. We honor reason in our tradition, and rebel against any faith system that demands we put aside our need for things to make sense. For others, The Light can represent the light of Spirit that ebbs and flows inside us as we feel sometimes drained and dusty, and other times energetic, enthusiastic, and supple. Some times in our lives are spirited times and others are dispirited times. As we contemplate the meanings of the dark times and the light times, the earth-based traditions would caution us against using The Dark as a symbol for all that is negative. If we use "darkness" to speak about ignorance, depression, and evil, we speak as if it would be best to have no darkness at all, to have light all the time. That would be awful. There is a season for dark and a season for light.

Is it possible then that there is a time to feel energetic and a time to feel drained in the rhythm of life? A time to let life and energy flow outward from you, and a time for it to flow inward? Maybe the ebb and flow of Spirit is a rhythm that is good to feel. Maybe in our growing into wholeness there is a time to feel dusty and dry, "hard as iron" like the winter ground, and stony as winter water. Maybe instead of worrying and suffering over those feelings we could settle into them, knowing that there is a time for cold and a time for warmth, a time to be energetic and a time to rest, a time to grow and a time to stay where you are, a time for the light of reason and a time for other ways of knowing. Maybe we could walk in beauty and balance more easily if we could welcome the dark time, trusting that when it reaches its full strength, things will begin their tilt back in the other direction. Nothing stays the same in the flow of things. All things seek their balance and their rhythm. The wheel will always turn. The light will always be reborn. We need not be afraid. This month, as humans have done for thousands of years, we can bid goodbye to The Dark in peace and greet the rebirth of The Light with rejoicing.

MEG BARNHOUSE

SICK AND SURLY

When I feel myself coming down with something I start emergency measures. I quit staying up late. I eat vitamins in just the right amount at just the right times. I drink eight glasses of water a day. I don't stop eating cheeseburgers, though. I've got to save something for when I am in serious trouble.

Mark Twain told the story of a virtuous man who died because he had no vices to give up. He fell sick and his doctor told him he had to give up alcohol to get better. "But, Doctor," he said, "I don't drink alcohol."

"Give up smoking, then."

"But, Doctor, I don't smoke!"

"Quit staying up all night at parties with wild women, then."

The sick man never did that either, and, having no vices to give up, he died. I'm keeping cheeseburgers in reserve.

For the run-of-the-mill kinds of sicknesses, I go to bed early, eat vitamins, drink water, and sip hot lemonade with honey. My mother used that remedy for just about everything.

It makes me mad to be sick. Somewhere I got the idea that sickness shouldn't happen. I don't plan for it in my world. I feel that my body should go on sturdily working like my '88 Accord, not making a fuss, never asking for too much attention.

In my family while I was growing up, we didn't mollycoddle our bodies. If you were really sick, you went to the hospital. If you weren't in the hospital you weren't really sick. Once my head hurt and my mother said, "Children don't get headaches." So I didn't get them anymore. At least, I didn't let myself acknowledge or even feel them. Allergies were more suspect than headaches. Adults would speak of it by deepening their voice and rolling their eyes: "Oh, you know, her son has—allergies." Imagine my surprise, a month after the birth of my first child, when I began itching all over my neck after patting the cat we'd had for the past six years. I had a vague feeling that something was morally wrong with me for having this allergy, so I felt itchy and guilty at the same time.

This past year I have been sick a lot. Not sick enough to go to the hospital, just sick enough to lie on the sofa looking pale and heroic. I don't know why I have been sick so much. I think it must be the karma fairy.

I have matured in compassion because the karma fairy has visited on me every single thing I used to look down on other people for having. You meet the karma fairy when, right after you curse righteously at someone who has cut in front of your car, you cut off someone else within the hour. You didn't see the other driver. It must be his fault. Your sneaking suspicion, though, is that you just did the very thing for which you were pouring contempt on someone else.

Now that the karma fairy has taught me about being sick, I'm more compassionate toward other people. Not to myself, though. I still get mad: *What?* I have to rest? I *hate* to rest. I might have to cancel appointments? Say it ain't so.

Someone may have to bring me hot lemonade and honey and pat my face and kiss my pale cheek? Well, okay. Just don't make me give up cheeseburgers.

MEG BARNHOUSE

While lying close to death in intensive care, with a dozen tubes stuck into my body—to drain me, to nourish me, to help me breathe, to monitor my heart—I was surprised by how much anger I felt. Later, when the things done to me made rational sense, as part of the regime to keep me alive, I was embarrassed by my anger. But at the time I merely raged inside.

One morning, I woke up and, for the first time after the surgery, looked around the room. One wall looked out on the nursing station in the hall. Ahead of me was a blank wall with only a darkened television set. I did not know what was behind me. I hadn't the strength to turn around.

In the fourth wall was the only window, which I assumed must look out on the green hills of Oregon. I did not know for sure because of a "thing" that blocked my view. "Isn't it just like this dumb hospital," I thought to myself. "The only window I can look out and they park this thing in the way."

Later I realized that the "thing" was the respirator that kept me breathing—and alive. I was angrier still with the rocking bed, which was to help me avoid pneumonia. How I hated that bed. Each time it rocked I was sure it would throw me out onto the cold floor. I found myself looking forward to the painful changing of dressings, merely because the bed would stop rocking.

After I became well, it occurred to me that the anger had been a good thing—one of the last struggles of my spirit to stay alive. I resolved to remember that lesson. In my dealings with angry people, it might help me to keep in mind that there is wisdom in anger even when there is not rationality. In my better moments I might try to see beyond red-faced anger to see what this suffering spirit might need so achingly.

BARBARA ROHDE

TO HOLD THE TEARS OF LOVE

On our last Sunday in Greece a few summers ago, we were awakened by church bells in the mountain village where we were staying. After breakfast on the sunny courtyard of the guesthouse, we drove down to Volos to see the museum.

In one room we stood beside the tomb of a six-year-old girl who had lived—and died—in the fourth century B.C.E. We looked at the things that had been placed in the stone coffin with her—a doll, a pair of sandals blackened by decay, a purple tunic, a small vessel to hold the tears of the mourners. Our guide told us that there was also evidence of food that had been left there—chestnuts, hazelnuts, apples, and pomegranates.

It seemed strange to feel a pang of sorrow for a death that had taken place twenty-four centuries ago, one death of an unknown child among anguished billions of deaths. But looking again at the small vial that had once held tears, it was clear that the pain was not for the child, but for those she had left behind, those who had placed the doll and the apple beside her in that final act of grief-struck love.

Something within us wanted to call out across vast fields of time and space, "We know. We know. All humans come to know. There is no vessel large enough to hold the tears of love."

BARBARA ROHDE

FIRE AT THE PARSONAGE

The fire started about midnight Saturday in the little storage room that connects the kitchen to the garage. To look into that burning room was to glimpse another world, a surprising alternate universe. It had always been an ordinary room I could walk in and out of, or through to the other side, without anything unusual happening. I was familiar with the contents of the room. I knew the texture and color of its surfaces. It had a certain smell and a certain sound.

This time when I opened the door I saw flames and swirling smoke that moved toward me and past me and stung my eyes and burned the inside of my nose. The universe had been orderly. Now, flowing out of that room into the rest of the world was chaos. Things were out of control. Destructive forces were loose.

The chief difference between the universe before and the universe after the opening of that door was in the dimension of time. I well know that all the things to which I am connected, loved ones, favored possessions, self, will be swept away in time. But the fire said: now. It may happen now.

The world is going to end, and we don't know when. My world, or yours, may end tomorrow in some unexpected way. Our shared world, earth's biosphere, will end as well; maybe ten million years from now when the sun overheats; maybe next week in an accidental nuclear war. We may have no warning, no time to prepare. Have we done what we need to do? Have we said the words we should say before the opportunity is gone?

The walls are cool now. The charred and water-soaked things are piled outside. The urgency has been replaced by weariness and aggravation. I remember that for a while I thought I knew exactly what was most important.

ROBERT R. WALSH

63

RETURNING FROM JORDAN HOSPITAL, EARLY OCTOBER

The red leaves shouted. I don't know how long
they worked at getting my attention. Eyes
on striped macadam, aimless thoughts of pain
and death and illness, issues of the self,
and selfless prayer—or was it just a wish?—
I blocked the sight without the aid of shades
or blinders.
   When the brightness hit me I
was stunned, a blow right to the soul, a K.O. to the
spiritual solar plexus. Here was transformation, all
creation, in its work ongoing, all around me. And
destruction, too, and death (forget them at your
peril). Eddying, splashing entropy was running to
the sea.
   A rest stop sign
appeared and I pulled off the road where I
could safely cry.

ROBERT R. WALSH

SOLSTICE

Night has its own kind of beauty,
    different than the beauty of day.
Night is a time of sleep and dreams and
    inward visions,
A time of pause within activity.
Darkness is an invitation to imagining and
    storytelling,
And to using ears instead of eyes to listen to the
    world in its stillness.
Darkness is the den of life in germination,
And darkness is the portal of death that opens
    to eternity:
The mystery of all time past and endless time
    to come.
At the center of our being
    there is light and there is darkness,
    the known and the unknown,
    the named and the nameless,
    the finite and the infinite.
Light and dark are different,
    but not opposed to each other.
Like a mother and father, they are friends with
    one another,
    and with us.

GARY A. KOWALSKI

SLAUGHTER OF INNOCENTS

According to the Gospel of Matthew, when King
Herod learned about the birth of Jesus, he ordered
the massacre of all male children under age two in
Bethlehem. This slaughter is still commemorated on
the Christian calendar with a feast day that falls
three days after Christmas.

By all historical accounts, Herod was a bloodthirsty
and heartless ruler. He killed his son five days before
his own death. Whether or not events happened just as
the Bible described them, they have the ring of truth,
sounding very much like the morning headlines.

Unfortunately, the slaughter of innocents is a daily
reality. Around the world, up to 100 million children
are exploited for their labor, sold into slavery and
prostitution, and forcibly recruited as cannon fodder
in armed conflicts. In our own country, children are
also abused. A hundred thousand go to bed homeless
each night. A quarter live in poverty. Many dwell in
urban war zones where drugs and violence numb the
mind and twist the spirit.

Amid the revelry of the holidays, let us not forget
the hungry and frightened children who are the
invisible witnesses to our feasting. Let us renew our
commitment to defending the weak and empower-
ing the powerless. And as we share our wishes for
peace on earth, let us remember that Herod is alive

and well today, wearing a three-piece suit or military uniform instead of a tunic or toga, but still the same old tyrant. Only the names have been changed—and not to protect the innocent.

GARY A. KOWALSKI

POEM IN A TIME OF PERIL

Of course truth is hard.
It is a rock.
Yet I do not think it will fall upon me
And crush me.
I do not think they can hammer it to bits
And stone me.

Help me place the rock in the strong current
Of these rushing waters.
I must climb upon it.
I must know how truth feels.
When I plunge naked
Into the bright depth of these waters,
I must know how truth feels.
When I am swept by the cold fury of these waters,
I must know, with my whole being, how truth feels.
I shall remember how truth feels.

I praise the rock.
I praise the river.
I fear the drought
More than death by water.

BARBARA ROHDE

THE COMING OF THE THAW

"Today if ye will hear his voice, harden not your heart."
—PSALMS 95:7-8

As a child I always thought the "hardened heart" of
the Bible meant the heart was frozen. To me it always
suggested sternness, cruelty, anger. Experience has
taught me that the slow coming of the ice is more
subtle, that there are times one doesn't recognize it
has happened until the moment of the thaw. Experience has taught me that this freezing often does not
reflect hostility or hatred, but a quieter kind of
defense—a defense against too much life, against the
possibility of pain, against self-knowledge.

Still, even in the quiet, there are signs—inertia or
frantic activity, boredom, self-pity, the failure to
respond authentically to the suffering of another,
even though one may go through the motions of
kindness. But when the thaw comes, it brings with it

the joy and pain of life restored. Life flows in us and through us. We are no longer exiled from ourselves.

And what can thaw us, open us into the fullness of our being? Like spring in Nebraska, the thaw can come as the strong warm power of the sun rising out of the darkness, or as the sudden breaking through the icy crust by the force of truth.

For me, at various times, it has been the wildness of Big Bend Park, or the ever-changing light of the skies of New Mexico, or the silver-gray Oregon Coast—the small loving act of a seeing friend, a sentence on a page shouting up at me, the solace of solitude or of the harmonies of music, a child's question, an artist's vision, a teacher's demand—those moments of real meaning, those moments when grief is accepted, those moments which cannot be defined except by the religious word "grace," when ordinary acts are lifted up to take on new meaning, and all of life becomes sacramental.

BARBARA ROHDE

PIETA

I

No love among the mourners. Let us cry.
Death came like a tear, something for the eyes
To lose, furrowing the face, bitter in the mouth,
Soft smallness without piety or fear.
And when we asked the headlines, they could only say:
At Buchenwald death crouched upon the floor;
Hiroshima found death could die no more.
They would be right and wrong. When
Is a useless question. Let us all ignore
Confusion and the clock. Let us call
Death death, not ask when death, or where.
Each finds the knowledge, lying in his bed.
Each raises shade to resurrect the sky
But finds no anger there, no penitence, no dread,
No love among the mourners. Let us cry.

II

Giotto knew. A scheme of light and shadow and
The understanding of a gentle hand.

Giotto knew. When Mary placed her arm across his
    breast,
The two embraced the pity of the rest.

Giotto knew abstractions have no breath
And brought to life by representing death.

No love among the mourners and a few
Must ask what lonely thing is dying. Giotto knew.

III
Like the chapel, his was no beautiful
Exterior. Bad jokes, six ugly children,
Even Dante laughed. His teacher found
Him drawing pictures in the dusty ground.
Freed from the cloister, what would the love
Be, the devout drama of the cross?
Giotto knew what pity was about.
Only his art would bring the inside out.

IV
No motion to accept or deny;
No love among the mourners. Let us cry.

(Written after a "sacred encounter" with a book on the Giotto frescoes, a book that also described the role Giotto played in bringing humanness into depictions of the divine.)

BARBARA ROHDE

THE ONE TRUTH

THE ONE TRUTH

I pray that for you there may be moments, perhaps minutes or even hours, of a larger awareness, a seeing through surfaces to essence.

Everything around you is a manifestation of a reality that is a unity.

It is there in the maple tree, in the polished beach stone, in the cumulus cloud.

It is there in the tilled soil, the clapboard siding, the comfortable chair.

It is in the child's laugh, the worker's sweat, your face in the mirror.

It is in the fear of war, the anger at injustice, the longing for love, the commitment to reconciliation.

The many truths spring from the one truth, and the beginning of wisdom is to open ourselves to the mystery of the one truth. May the moments of awareness be there in your days, and in mine, too.

ROBERT R. WALSH

A NONALOGUE FOR THE FRIDGE

A friend asked me to try my hand at rewriting the Ten Commandments. She wanted something to tape to the door of the fridge.

I only came up with nine. But then I spent much less time on this than it took Moses to climb the mountain.

1. You shall not worship the finite and the conditional as if it were the ultimate.
2. You shall keep to a rhythm of work and rest in the spirit of the sabbath.
3. You shall keep your promises.
4. You shall tell the truth.
5. You shall try to make amends for the things you break.
6. You shall honor the people who give and sustain life.
7. You shall honor the earth.
8. You shall grant to others the same rights to life, liberty, and property that you claim for yourself.
9. You shall be kind.

ROBERT R. WALSH

SWEET SUNDAY

My favorite Sabbaths as a child were when my brother and I went with my father to deliver frankfurters and ground beef to the food stand at the amusement park down the street from my father's meat market. The park was one of my favorite places. I loved the merry-go-round, the Tunnel of Love, the Ferris wheel. My mother wouldn't let us ride the roller coaster—there had been too many accidents—but I loved the sound of the wheels on the tracks getting faster and faster and the screams of the people getting louder and louder. Sometimes during the summer, when the wind was just right, I could lie in bed and hear the screams from the roller coaster and the music from the merry-go-round or the dance hall. I thought it was my own special lullaby.

There was something grandly mysterious about being in the park on a Sunday morning when everything was quiet, when we were the only visitors. There was a marvelous sense of waiting, of being in the middle of a deep sleep just before everything awakens. While my father settled the bill with the man at the food stand, my brother and I would run around the park, watching the monkeys in their cages, running from horse to horse on the merry-go-round, or looking at the motionless Ferris wheel, the parked bumper cars, the towering architecture of the roller coaster tracks. It was as if the park was filled with the spirits of people who had been there or were yet to come. But for the moment we were there alone, as if the entire place had been created just for us.

When my father called us, we ran back to the stand. The man who worked there gave us each a candied apple covered with coconut. My father suggested we sit on a bench under one of the maple trees while we ate our apples-on-a-stick.

In the years since I left home I have been in many holy places, from the cathedrals at Canterbury and Chartres to the rim of the Grand Canyon, but I am not sure any were as sacred as that quiet amusement park on summer Sunday mornings in Nebraska. In my heart I am always there, tasting the crispness of apple mingled with the sweetness of sugar syrup and the crunchiness of white coconut, the dappled sunlight touching my face, my father's arm around me, and the entire park waiting there with us, ready to awaken and be filled with life.

BARBARA ROHDE

THE MIRACULOUS PITCHER

During the hot Nebraska summers of my childhood, I spent hours, high in my treehouse, devouring the books I found in the small collection my parents had acquired from the estates of various relatives.

One of my favorites was *A Wonder Book,* Nathaniel Hawthorne's retelling of classical myths. My favorite of those stories was "The Miraculous Pitcher," the story of Baucis and Philemon. This elderly, poor, but generous-hearted couple invite two gods, disguised as beggars, to come into their cottage to rest and eat. The gods keep asking that their bowls be replenished, and the old couple become sad and embarrassed because they know the pitcher is empty. But the gods show them otherwise. No matter how often they pour from the pitcher, it is always full.

I suppose that as a child, what I liked was the thought of possessing such a pitcher. Much later I realized that in some sense I did. The story of the miraculous pitcher seems to be telling us that in the realm of the spirit there is no such thing as a non-renewable resource.

That is an important concept. Most of us have it backward. For centuries we have had it backward. We have believed that material resources are infinite but the resources of the spirit need to be hoarded with care. We act as if the supply of oil can go on forever but that there are limits to the amount of love we can give away. How often I have found myself closing off from people in need because I was afraid of being spiritually drained, only to find myself in the driest of deserts.

We have arrived at a time in our history when we are beginning to realize that this planet is our only home; we can no longer make a mess of the place where we are and then move on. A species can come to an end. Resources can be used up. All growth is not a sign of health.

But I suspect we doubt more than ever the truth in the story of the miraculous pitcher—or the loaves and the fishes. We find it hard to believe that we will find the spiritual nourishment to meet the needs of this chaotic age.

The wisdom of the centuries and our own experience tell us otherwise. If we do not let our fears have dominion, we may discover that in the midst of pain we find inner strength, in the midst of bewilderment we find inner clarity, in the midst of nourishing another we find ourselves nourished.

BARBARA ROHDE

TOGETHER IN THE MAZE

Camping our way through Europe when our children were small, my husband and I were persuaded by the chorus of their eager voices to take them to the maze at Hampton Court, just outside of London. We drove there one summer afternoon and started exploring, each of us separately walking along the hedge-lined paths.

Often I could hear a recognizable voice on the other side of the hedge or would meet a familiar face coming back from a blind alley, as we searched the paths with a group of strangers—some laughing, some anxious, some impatient—all of us together in this puzzle. Suddenly the meaning of what we were doing seemed to expand beyond the paths we were walking, into our lives.

When I finally reached the center of the maze and found people sitting on benches in the sun, quietly talking, laughing, sharing apples out of a backpack, it was with a mixture of surprise and recognition— surprise because I had had it in my head that a maze was something to get through rather than to find the center of—recognition, partly because I had once seen a diagram of Hampton Court, but primarily because the experience seemed "true" in some way.

I remembered how that morning I had pored over the guidebook worrying about whether we would have time to do all the sights in the few days remaining. I remembered sorrowfully leaving my favorite Botticelli painting because of the strange sense of obligation to see as many rooms of the museum as I could.

Many times in the years since that lovely August day that memory has come back to me. When I find myself hurrying through an experience, trying to solve or finish it rather than immersing myself in it and giving full attention to the moment, I often remember the maze. Then I remind myself, "It is the center you are looking for, that timeless moment in the noonday sun."

BARBARA ROHDE

GRADUATION

Ever since I graduated from college, I have had a recurring dream. My wife has had it, too, as well as a lot of other people I know. In my dream, it is time to take an exam and I am unprepared. I have not gone to classes all semester. I failed to do the reading. Usually, I am even a little confused about the subject matter. What was being taught? Who was teaching? What was I supposed to learn? No answers are provided. Now it is too late to make up for lost time. With a sense of approaching catastrophe, I realize that although I am about to be tested, I haven't a clue how to pass.

What is the meaning of this peculiar dream? I was never that nervous about taking tests in real life, because I was a fairly good student. Why does it seem to be a fixture of our collective unconscious? Surely it concerns something more than lingering classroom jitters.

I think it is a dream about the Great Examination
that each of us must face. The items on the exam are
the Ultimate Questions: Who am I? What do I want?
What am I afraid of? To whom (or what) am I com-
mitted? Where is my own highest good calling me?

This is not just a dream about academic anxieties
or forgetting the dates of the Magna Carta. It is
about forgetting our own reason for being.

We have one lifetime (that we know about), and
no make-ups are allowed. Is it any wonder we are all
tossing and turning in our sleep? By the time
morning comes, we have to be ready to give some
account of ourselves. Sooner or later, we have to
answer for how we choose to spend our lives.

GARY A. KOWALSKI

A LIFE WELL SPENT

One night I heard an old man say, "I had a wasted
life." I began wondering what it would take for me
to say I had wasted my life. I could have lived a life
where I only watched TV and cleaned my house.
Then I would lie on my death bed and remember
my life while wailing and gnashing my teeth in that
clean, clean house. I could have been a company
woman making six figures and working 60 hours a

week, too busy for my family, my church, my garden, and taking small comfort in remembering that I had never missed a day of work.

As I lie on my death bed, what do I want to remember? Right now my relationship with my father is painful. I asked him four or five years ago to stop quoting the Bible to me because it made me feel like throwing up and screaming. He stopped immediately, even though the Bible is his reference, his rule, and his delight. We continue to talk every two or three months, but he has less and less to say. I don't know what I want to do about it. Part of me wants to give up. It would be a relief to surround myself only with people who are like-minded.

I don't want to remember being cut off from my father because he doesn't talk to me the way I would like him to talk to me. I don't want to look back on drifting away from my family because they are devoted Christians and I am Christian in ethics and Pagan in practice.

In *The Wheel of Life*, people told Elizabeth Kubler-Ross that when they went toward the Light, they were shown how all our lives are intertwined. Our actions and thoughts affect the Universe like ripples in a pond. People reported hearing the question: "What service have you rendered?" The Light asked them to consider whether they had made the highest and best choices in life, and whether they had learned the ultimate lesson of unconditional love.

I wish I hadn't read that passage. I'm not great at unconditional love. I try, but lots of people annoy me. Even when I have the time, attention, and patience to love unconditionally, I'm not sure what it involves. I know it doesn't mean being sweet and dewey-eyed and telling people they are wonderful no matter what. I know unconditional love involves disagreement and challenge. So how do I know, in each situation, what unconditional love involves?

What would be a life well spent for a regular, somewhat irresponsible, but often charming person without a lot of moral fortitude like myself? I heard one woman say she just wanted to live long enough to grow every kind of tulip there was. Another friend said she wanted to live long enough to see her daughter struggle with a seventeen-year-old daughter just like her.

What would satisfy me? I will be glad if I have raised my children with honesty and love; if I have made music with other people; if I have seen beauty and loved it; if I have learned how to get along with my relatives; if I have made a soul connection with Spirit, friends, and lovers; and if I have claimed my right to tell the truth as I see it. Oh, and I want to be wonderful. That's all.

MEG BARNHOUSE

DÉJÀ VU

In a wonderful essay called "Once More To the Lake," the late E. B. White described how he spent a week one summer with his son at a fishing camp in Maine. He had passed time there as a boy many years before, swimming, canoeing, and exploring the woods. Revisiting the site, he experienced the strange sensation that he had become his own father, and that he and his son were merely re-enacting scenes from his own remembered past.

"I seemed to be living a dual existence," he wrote. "I would be in the middle of some simple act, I would be picking up a bait box or laying down a table fork, or I would be saying something, and suddenly it would be not I but my father saying the words or making the gesture. It gave me a creepy sensation." The smell of pine in the morning air, the drone of insects at evening, the sound of oars squeaking in rusty locks combined to create the illusion that time repeated itself, or stood still, so that eternity was present in each trance-like hour.

I often have that same sensation of living a life that has been lived before. When I look into my children's eyes and see my own image, I feel as if I am merely a channel for the stream of life that has coursed through countless generations. If we find transcendence anywhere, it is here and now, in the reverie of a summer day, or listening, like people long before us, and like those who will follow, to the slow sigh of trees bending in the night breeze.

"Summertime, oh summertime," E. B. White exclaimed, "pattern of life indelible, the fadeproof lake, the woods unshatterable, the pasture with the sweetfern and the juniper forever and ever. . . ."

There is only one thing to do at the lake, and that is to dive in headfirst. The quiet depths will swallow us, but also give us life.

GARY A. KOWALSKI

KNOTS

My daughter Holly, who is six, recently learned to tie her shoes. It was a challenge she had been struggling with for many months, and her sense of accomplishment was evident. It also gave me a sense of pride, because I had helped teach her.

After many failed and frustrating attempts to show her how the knot was made, the technique that finally succeeded was simple. Instead of sitting in front of Holly, facing her, I moved behind her, reaching around from the back to manipulate the laces on her shoe so that we shared the same "angle of vision" on the problem. My hands were in the same position as hers instead of reversed, and that made it easy for her to grasp what needed to be done.

It occurred to me how many other problems are like that. Whether we are trying to communicate some concept, resolve a conflict, or explain a new idea, the trick is to see the situation from the other person's point of view. "The way to persuade someone," columnist Sydney Harris once observed, "is not to beckon him to come and look at things from where *you* stand, but to move over to where *he* stands and try to walk hand in hand to where you would like both of you to stand." Solutions that eluded us before then become almost self-evident. Resistance melts away.

If you want to change the world, understanding how it looks to other folks is crucial. Even for more knotty problems, like learning how to tie shoes, empathy is one of the most powerful tools there is.

GARY A. KOWALSKI

SHADOW AND LIGHT

A nurse came into the Tennessee hospital room where I was visiting an old friend. My friend introduced us. "Well," said the nurse, upon hearing that I am a minister, "see what you think of this."

She took an object from her pocket, unwrapped it from several layers of plastic film, and handed it to me. It was a photograph. She explained that a friend of hers wanted a picture of Hurricane Hugo; he had gone out toward the end of the storm and taken a snapshot.

The picture showed a dark area of sky and some white clouds. She said, "What do you think of that?"

I searched for something of interest in the picture. I said, gamely, "It looks a little like Pac-Man." She said, "Look in the upper right corner."

I looked in the upper right corner and still saw nothing but clouds and sky. I thought, this hurricane caused immense destruction; maybe she sees a source of evil in these clouds. I looked for horns or a pitchfork or a pointy tail. Fortunately, I made no comment until she spoke again.

"It's Christ," she said.

She pointed. "There's his hand. There's his robe. . . ." Then the shape emerged and I saw what she wanted me to see. I acknowledged to her that I could now see it.

She said, "Well, what do you think of that?" Still not knowing what was expected of me, I said nothing. She said, "It's like he's pointing and saying, 'See what I can do?'" I said, "Hmm."

The nurse took the picture back, wrapped it in the plastic, pocketed it, and repeated, "It's like he's saying, 'See what I can do?'" She left the room.

She and I looked at the same pattern of shadow and light. She saw a vision of power in the hands of a figure of healing and forgiveness. I saw a vision of power that was chaotic and destructive—and that set me looking for the source of evil.

We were each grasping a part of the truth.

ROBERT R. WALSH

A MAN'S PRAYER

I am wondrously wrought: partly shaped by my biology, partly shaped by my culture, and partly self-shaped.

I am so wonderfully fashioned that the workings of my self amaze and confuse me.

I know I have the power to choose among many paths, yet most of the time I am on automatic pilot, acting out of little-examined assumptions, values, rituals, myths, appetites, and impulses.

I can meet life in many ways:

I can be tough-minded; I can be tender-hearted.

I can move between activity and quietness.

I can express my uniqueness and individuality, and I can forget myself in commitment to family and community.

I can judge, I can bear witness to the good and the evil around me; and I can forgive.

I can analyze, theologize, figure the world out; and I can listen to the still small voice of conscience, intuition, the holy spirit.

All these ways of meeting life, and more, are part of the potential that is me. But I am afraid to move very far or very fast from the ways that have become comfortable.

I seek the self-knowledge that may illuminate new possibilities in life, and I seek the courage to try them.

Most of all I pray for wholeness, for a life in which my many ways of living can be connected and filled with the meaning of holy Creation.

ROBERT R. WALSH

THE POET GOD

God is writing a poem.
I am one of the words.
He utters me.

(Do I mean what He means me to mean?)

When God's voice stops,
When the poem is finished,
The poem will be.
I will be.

(Do you think poems die? They are completed.
Do you think we die? We complete the poem.)

Without me, the poem would not be whole.
Without the poem, my word is hollow sound.
Without God, nothing.

(The world goes mad with noise.
We cannot hear ourselves.
God, sing in our ears again.)

BARBARA ROHDE

A NEW YEAR

I once actually greeted the new year in Times Square.
It was the beginning of 1954, when I was sixteen. We
stayed at the Hotel Taft. The orchestra of Vincent
Lopez was playing in the Taft ballroom, and I danced
with my mother. Times Square was cold, crowded,
brightly lit, noisy, and exciting. People spoke to
strangers and wished them well. At midnight I was at
the center of the world and at the center of time. I
had no sense of fear in Times Square.

I remember feeling that the discontinuity at the
turn of the year was real, that time stopped at
midnight and then started again, that the new year
with its new number was really new.

Now my parents are gone, Vincent Lopez is gone, Times Square has become a different kind of place, and to my grown-up instincts the city at midnight brings a sense of danger. I have danced and sung and hugged and kissed through many a New Year's Eve. I have made new beginnings, good ones, although I think none of them happened on a January 1st.

I wish for you in this new year as many new beginnings as you need, and no more than you can handle. May they come not at a particular turn of the calendar page or striking of the clock, but just when you need them.

In this year, may you remember old acquaintances, and may peace break out, even if only a little bit, in the world, and in your life.

ROBERT R. WALSH

AND THE RIVER FLOWS ON

"As long as there are otters in the river, you know everything is all right." That's what a bereaved father told me shortly after his little girl died. Emily was only three. She had been ill and feverish and then one night simply stopped breathing. It was finished before the ambulance arrived, and there was nothing anyone could have done differently to prevent or forestall her death. It was just one of those unavoidable, unaccountable sorrows the universe sometimes lays upon us.

I was meeting with Emily's father to plan her memorial service. He hoped to scatter her ashes near a nature trail that had been recently constructed near a local river. It was comforting to think of otters swimming and playing there, frolicking in the sun and mostly innocent of the kind of grief we humans have to suffer.

Other animals had recently returned to the river after a long absence, and their presence meant the river was clean. The run-off from the soil in the surrounding country was relatively free of harmful chemicals. The rain was not too acidic for fish or shellfish to live there. Nature was working as it should, keeping birth and death in a balance that changed with each season and evolved through time, but rested on a reassuring dependability that life would go on. So even in a world where three year olds sometimes get sick and die, one might still have faith in an order that underlies creation.

This natural order doesn't take away the pain. But it does help me to know that while the world is full of grief, it remains full of wet, splashing, animal gladness. The river claims us all, and the river flows on. So long as there are otters, you know that somehow, everything may be all right.

GARY A. KOWALSKI

GOING TO AN INNER PARTY

I don't know if you have this experience, but I find overheard conversations are more interesting than the ones I'm part of. Television sounds more interesting if I don't catch exactly what's being said; an unopened Christmas present is always better than an opened one; the inventions I think up while half asleep are more fabulous than the ones my waking mind comes up with; and what's about to happen is more interesting than what's happening now. The thoughts along the edges of the mainstream are more interesting than the ones in full consciousness.

I don't know what to call it when mis-reading and mis-hearing things are a source of inspiration and delight. Right now I think of it as my inner poet. I picture her as a tricky laughing woman who's cross-eyed from trying to see around corners.

Here's what I'm talking about: I heard someone on the radio say faintly, "It's coming in at the speed of snow." I still don't know what they really said, but who cares? "It's coming in at the speed of snow" is something you'd hear in a dream. What exactly is the speed of snow? It's a Zen koan. The imagination opens and the linear train of thought derails.

Rereading something I had written the other day, I found a typo. I was talking about a dinner party and I had left off the "d." Going to an "inner party" sounds fun, although I'm not sure how you'd get there, who would be invited, and what would be served. I'm pretty sure you'd get to dance, though, and I think once in a while I've heard the music.

Driving home from the mountains one afternoon, I saw a sign for the Trinity Fish Camp. When I looked again it said Tri-city Fish Camp, but I think "trinity" is a better name. After all, Jesus was a fisherman, and because one member of the trinity spent a lot of time fishing, I think it's an apt name. You can picture the disciples at the Trinity Fish Camp, sitting around a paper-covered table cracking crabs and talking theology, hush-puppy crumbs in their beards.

Another time I thought I saw a sign that said Children's Truck Stop, and I got to thinking what a children's truck stop might be like. Would children bring their trucks, gas them up, get the windshields washed? Would they buy tiny boots and eat small burgers with pecan swirls for dessert? I know there would be video games.

I love the flickering things that bump along the edges of mainstream consciousness. These glimpses of an inner wisdom flash like fish in a creek, and if I can grab one by the tail I feel like I have a treasure. I'll keep fishing for them, and I'll share them with you. But right now I've got to go. I'm off to an inner party at the speed of snow.

MEG BARNHOUSE

FIREWORKS

Starbursts explode at midnight
And vanish like a year gone by.
Pinwheels whirl,
Seasons spin,
And sputter to an end.
In this fierce and fleeting world
We celebrate
Our birth and death,

New creation and the passing of the old.
For like a flare,
We live by burning,
And what is consumed is that which gives light.
So let us burn brightly,
And not begrudge what is spent,
But let the pyrotechnics engulf us,
Like roman candles blazing,
Or sparklers in the night.

GARY A. KOWALSKI

FATHER'S DAY

Sometimes I fool my children. I take a bright coin, put it in one ear, then pretend to take it out the other side, and they think I'm the greatest magician in the world. Other times I like to take three oranges and see how long I can juggle them. Usually I drop the oranges after two or three throws, but Holly and Noah still think I'm the best juggler around. I deceive my children in other ways, too. I let them think that I'm the smartest Dad in the world, as well as the strongest. And I also tell them that I'm the big boss at the church where I am the minister, which is perhaps the largest fib of all. Someday they'll learn the truth.

The truth is that I'm not the smartest or the strongest or the best juggler or the big boss. I don't know how to knit or fix airplanes. And when they find that out, I hope my kids still love and respect me. Because each of us needs to be loved, and the greatest feeling in the world is to know that other people think you're special, even though you can't pull rabbits out of hats.

You see, not everyone can astonish their friends with sleight of hand. Not everyone can be Number One, Chief Executive, or at the top of their field. But each one of us can be the world's best Dad in the eyes of our children. The amazing thing is that there is enough love for everyone, and the more we share the more we have. That's the real magic.

GARY A. KOWALSKI

HARVEST

The last tomatoes in the garden are clinging to the vine, doing their best to ignore the change in season. It is my neighbor's garden, and because these are not my tomatoes, I can afford to be philosophical about them.

It occurs to me that the basic strategy of these vegetables is a mistaken one. The biological winners will be those that accepted their fall with grace weeks ago, when the ground was still warm and welcoming. Next year they will be the ones to produce new seedlings.

What is it, I wonder, that keeps these last fruits hanging on? Is it hope? Fortitude? Perseverance? Or just a bad sense of timing?

Timing is essential to the art of living: knowing when to hang in there and when to let go, when to struggle and when to surrender, knowing how to recognize the seasonable changes of our lives.

May we be blessed with the wisdom of good gardens.

GARY A. KOWALSKI

A GOOD AGE

I don't mind being fifty. It seems a good age to me. There is much joking around big birthdays in mid-life, but there's often a sick quality to it. It is humor that plays off a fear of aging. This is the dominant theme in humorous birthday cards. The people who manufacture these cards know what they're doing: they're capitalizing on a fear that is deep in our collective psyche.

We would enjoy life a lot more if we could accept the things that are given and just worry about the things we can influence. What does it profit us to deny our age?

Don't get me wrong—I grieve over the losses I have suffered in the passing of time. I am angry and frustrated about the parts of my body that don't work as well as they used to. For example, my eyes. Oh, for the days when, unassisted, I could read my digital wristwatch and then look up and read a distant traffic sign!

But needing bifocals and being fifty are two different things. They may go together, they may not. Some people are born with poor eyesight, and some never need glasses. Loss of good vision is bad, but being fifty is good.

So let us try to eat properly and exercise and get enough sleep and stay interested in the world. Let us rage at the losses of family and friends and muscle tone and organic functioning, and at the pain. But let us realize that it is good, very good, to be exactly the age we are.

ROBERT R. WALSH

INTERRUPTION

On US-30, west of Gettysburg, I saw a dead deer beside the road. I sped on past. I had hundreds of miles to go that day. Then I felt called back. I made a U-turn on the four-lane highway and returned to the deer.

It was early on a Sunday morning. There was little traffic.

I approached and crouched beside the body. His eyes were open. I imagined for a moment that he was still alive, but there was no movement, no breath. I had been drawn to the deer by reverence and awe, but these gave way initially to curiosity and amateur forensic analysis.

One of his hind legs was broken, with the bone sticking out. There was a pool of dark blood under his head. There was a trail of blood about thirty feet long from the near lane of the highway. There were bony stubs where his antlers had been. I guessed he had been hit by a car, had died of a head injury, and had been dragged by someone to the shoulder of the road. I guessed the antlers had been taken for souvenirs.

I touched his side, his face, his broken leg. I sat with him for a minute or two, then decided to move him off the shoulder and into the underbrush. I pulled him by his forelegs, dragging him over and down a six-foot bank. I covered him with large leaves of weeds that grew there.

I said a prayer. I apologized for the system, my system, of people and machines and roads that had brought his meaningless death. I apologized for the indifference, which I have shared, that had brought his mutilation. I gave thanks for having found the courage to stop and to touch him.

I returned to my car and resumed my journey south.

ROBERT R. WALSH

AUTUMN ALERT

I have just returned from the northern woods and I bring alarming news. Something there is turning the leaves to red and gold . . . and it's coming this way.

Already here one can see signs. An unfamiliar coolness in the air. Sailboats being brought in. Just this morning a school bus went by.

Take warning, friends. Every leaf in our fair town is doomed, and every green unfinished summer dream will now be foreclosed. We have had our fleeting summertime.

ROBERT R. WALSH

The light green shoots of blossoms-to-have-been are out of sight under the drifting snow. Gale force winds are rattling the old house. The temperature is far below freezing. Nature is not cooperating with preparations for Easter.

The storm evokes the spiritual quality of Good Friday more than Easter. New life will appear, but not without strife, not without some losses to the coldness which returns as inevitably as spring. And who can say that the sun will always climb again on Easter morning? Isn't it at least possible that the coldness has more staying power than the warmth?

The seasons are more reliable in these matters than human nature. For we, individually and collectively, can choose between love and indifference, between commitment and self-absorption, between peace and war. And we have often chosen the coldness.

Maybe the ancients were right. Maybe the spring comes because we bid it to come in our celebrations. Maybe it is the telling and the retelling of the stories that enable us to see that hope still lives and that we can carry it forward.

The stories make it clear that God does not do it alone. The motions of the spheres will produce a sunrise, but the springtime of the spirit, the springtime of love and justice and peace, depends on our human response to the gift of life.

Let us tell the stories again.

ROBERT R. WALSH

SOLVENTS

They've discovered that Michelangelo originally painted the Sistine Chapel ceiling in bright colors, and some people are upset about it.

When we visited the Vatican they were about three-quarters through with the big cleaning job on the ceiling. The restorers were working from a bridge-like scaffold designed much like Michelangelo's, using the same mounting holes in the walls. As the cleaning was done, the scaffold was moved down the length of the ceiling. The movement was in reverse primordial time, starting with the flood and moving toward the creation.

Someone said the scaffold was like a very slow windshield wiper. In front of it the frescoes were dull and gloomy. Behind it they were clear and bold. We were among the first people in several centuries to see those bright colors. The almost-touching fingers of God and Adam were just visible on the clean side of the scaffold. It looked wonderful.

There are art critics who claim that Michelangelo was a gloomy fellow who deliberately added a layer of dullness over the bright paints after the plaster dried. In their view, the solvents are removing not only soot and smoke, but part of the original artwork. So we are now seeing colors the artist did not intend us to see.

Well, maybe he wasn't so gloomy. I'm no expert, but I prefer the new Michelangelo.

It is officially spring now. Here and there we see a drop of primary color in a gray timescape. A cardinal. A crocus. A momentary flood of bright light. Soon the sun will drive the dullness away and the greenness and blueness and yellowness of the earth and the sky will spread out all around us.

I wonder if I am ready for spring within myself. I think I have some residue to clean away, deposited by the candles burned through long nights. I think I know what the solvents are: sunlight, children, music, prayer, true meetings with people, hands to hold.

ROBERT R. WALSH

THE TIMELESS LUNCH

I had lunch with a person who had just passed her second birthday. Her vocabulary included ketchup, salt, pickle, mustard, and spoon—but she could not yet name the Worcestershire sauce. She could count to ten with confidence—but when she got into the teens she began to rattle off numbers at random. Her curiosity was boundless. I knew that her knowledge of the world would grow apace, and her ability to manipulate the symbols of language would expand.

I thought, the little person I see before me, lining up the restaurant condiments and counting and naming them, exists only for this moment. Even in the course of this meal she is growing and changing. If I meet her again in a month, she will be learning something else, and saying other words. She—and I—will have left this day behind.

I knew that the moment I had across the table from her was irreplaceable. There could be no other meeting between that particular her and that particular me. The experience could not be saved up or stored. So I was there with her as she spooned milk into the mouth of her stuffed bear.

And I think I loved her, when she held my hand as her mother unlocked the car.

ROBERT R. WALSH

ASSIGNMENT

While I am away, here are some things I want you to do. I want you to take care of yourself. Button up your overcoat. Fasten your seat belt. Eat your vegetables.

I want you to take care of someone else. Look for ways to help. Say, "I love you" (if you do). Hug a friend.

I want you to take care of your soul. Keep the different parts of your self in touch with one another. Listen for quiet clues about the path your life should be following. Be aware of what kind of world you are helping to make each day.

Take good care.

ROBERT R. WALSH

ABOUT THE AUTHORS

Meg Barnhouse is a pastoral counselor and the minister of the Unitarian Universalist Church of Spartanburg, South Carolina. She also holds a black belt in karate.

Gary A. Kowalski is a life-long Unitarian Universalist who has served as the minister for congregations in Kent, Washington, and Burlington, Vermont. He is the author of *The Souls of Animals, Goodbye Friend*, and *The Bible According to Noah*. He and his wife Dori have two children, one dog, and five chickens.

Barbara Rohde was an active lay Unitarian Universalist and community leader in Corvallis, Oregon, for forty years. She was also a political activist and author who inspired her daughter Kate to become a Unitarian Universalist minister. She died in 2001.

Robert R. Walsh is the minister of First Parish Church Unitarian Universalist in Duxbury, Massachusetts. He plays the five-string banjo and has three children and four grandchildren.

ALSO FROM SKINNER HOUSE BOOKS

Day of Promise: Collected Meditations, Volume One. Collected by Kathleen Montgomery.

An anthology of one hundred meditations from more than forty authors. ISBN 1-55896-419-3.

What We Share: Collected Meditations, Volume Two. Collected by Patricia Frevert.

Meditations from Richard S. Gilbert, Bruce T. Marshall, Elizabeth Tarbox, and Lynn Ungar. ISBN 1-55896-423-1.

Listening for Our Song: Collected Meditations, Volume Four. Collected by Margaret L. Beard.

Meditations from David S. Blanchard, Jane Ranney Rzepka, Elizabeth Tarbox, Sarah York. Available Fall 2002. ISBN 1-55896-438-X.